SHOUTING AT AN EMPTY HOUSE

SHOUTING AT AN EMPTY HOUSE

POEMS

DAVID B. PRATHER

Sheila-Na-Gig Editions

ISBN: 979-8-9873058-8-1
Library of Congress Control Number: 2023943104

Sheila-Na-Gig Editions
Russell, KY
Hayley Mitchell Haugen, Editor
www.sheilanagigblog.com

Advance Praise

Yeats advised poets to "Think like a wise man but communicate in the language of the people." There is much wisdom in this splendid collection, and it is rendered wholly accessible by the poet's ability to communicate plainly with his audience. With precise verbal skill and meticulous detail, Prather presents a rare clarity into the mysteries surrounding our everyday lives, our personal and collective histories, noticing and knowing the extraordinary in the ordinary, telling our stories with "one long and lingering breath." These are stunning poems, delivered by a poet in love with poetry, and ultimately, with us.

—Kirk Judd, author of *My People Was Music*

Shouting at an Empty House invites you to ponder what the poet hears echoing from this neo-pastoral lamentation breaking into Appalachian prayer. Does he "wish the whole world" feels "this kind of joy," as in the poem "Apple Snowfall?" These poems are topographical, the way they look down on the past, where "someone who would take us as we are, / never asks whether or not we are ready to go," from the poem, "Expulsion." With the lyrical simplicity of an Amish heretic, who asks if he's "been dismissed from Paradise," the intimacy of transcendence is covered in dirt framing the narrative of this stunning collection. Let him do to you what his poems ask the world, "Replace" your "heart with an apple."

—Daniel Edward Moore, author of *Waxing the Dents*

Acknowledgments

Some of these poems appeared in slightly different forms when they originally appeared in publication.

The American Journal of Poetry: "Learning to Fish the Little Kanawha"
American Literary Review: "Continuity"
Amethyst Review: "Eve's Theme"
Bluestone Review: "Ascension"
California Quarterly: "Tatterdemalion"
Cutleaf: "Not a Sonnet," "The Boy in the High School Science Room"
Cutthroat, A Journal of the Arts: "Associative"
Dickinsonian: "Lynnette, Early Spring, 1979"
The Ekphrastic Review: "Living with What I Cannot Find"
Furious Gazelle: "Mythological," "The Nubbins"
Grey Sparrow Journal: "Crows or Ravens," "Early Spring Disciples"
Gyroscope Review: "Compensatory"
I Thought I Heard a Cardinal Sing: Ohio's Appalachian Voices, Sheila-Na-Gig
    Editions, "Crows or Ravens"
Lullwater Review: "Ode to August in the Northern Hemisphere"
Neologism: "Barometer"
North/South Appalachia: "Mid-Season in Zone Six"
Northern Appalachia Review: "The Plight of Frankenstein's Monster"
Pandemic Evolution: Poets Respond to the Art of Matthew Wolfe, Sheila-Na-
    Gig Editions, "Out of Alignment"
Pangolin Review: "After the Storm" (as "The Expulsion"), "Hyperbole,"
    "Resuscitation"
Pif Magazine: "Unmoored"
Potomac Review: "Elliptical Orbit," "Round Trip"
Red Tree Review: "Umbra"
Ripe Literary Journal: "Zeptosecond"
River Heron Review: "Contrapuntal"
RockPaperPoem: "In Decline"
Rumble Fish Quarterly: "August Everywhere"
San Antonio Review: "Waiting for the Coming Storm"
Scarlet Leaf Review: "Four Years After Surgery," "Lost Youth,"
    "Ontological," "The Zombie"

Sharing This Delicate Bread: Selections from Sheila-Na-Gig online 2016-2021, Sheila-Na-Gig Editions, "Expulsion"

Sheila-Na-Gig online: "Almanac," "Apple Snowfall," "Expulsion"

South Florida Poetry Journal: "Diurnal," "(Omen) The Neighborhood of Make Believe" (as "The Neighborhood of Make Believe")

Sparks of Calliope: "On the Occasion of Solemnity"

Spider Mirror Journal: "Blight"

Still: The Journal: "Humidity," "If a Tree Falls in the Forest"

Verse-Virtual: "Fire Song," "A Prediction of Rain," "The Size of Myth"

voice lux journal: "Narcissism"

Voices from the Fierce Intangible World: An Anthology of Poets from the First 10 Issues of South Florida Poetry Journal SoFloPoJo, SoFloPoJo Press, "Diurnal"

West Trade Review: "Architecture for Elephants"

Wild Word Magazine: "Provenance"

Notes:

In "Diurnal," the phrase, *You forget and you forget*, is from the poem "The Sundays of Satin Legs Smith" by Gwendolyn Brooks.

Contents

1

2

3

for my sister

1

~ Waiting centuries for someone to tell our story ~

Apple Snowfall

—for Susan Sheppard

I don't know if you can feel the breeze
            where you are right now,
but it is frisky in the limbs of apple trees

and scatters all those loose petals.
        It is a storm. Pale purple

ground ivy blooms raise a fanfare
deep in the shadows of others.
I wish the whole world felt

this kind of joy. A quick gust
tickles branches, and a floral squall

                flutters and flows.
Can you feel the ecstasy? Can you feel
that lingering chill in the air?

        This is one of those days
that reminds me of the struggle to change,

of the way one loss leads to another.
And, still, there will be a harvest.
            Bees in rapture

spiral through the faint, sweet scent.
        Listen to me—the *faint,*

sweet scent. I wish
            you were here with me
to feel the tug and pull of the cat's-paw wind

batting at my sleeves, running around my legs.
I wish you could have met my friend,

      gone now,

who could have told us what it means
when apple trees toss their blossoms like brides,
if it means anything at all.

Almanac

Robins, I've been told, are harbingers of spring.
Or should I say something more positive?

Should I say bringer or messenger
or lover? No.

These birds tell lies, showing up at the end
of winter, promising early warmer weather,

drawing us all out of doors unjustly.
Unjustly. Even now,

robins flinch and flutter in wisteria twigs.
They can't know the trickery of frost,

the foolishness of buds come too early.
So much has come too early.

How could anyone trust old wives' tales?
Even the old wives are gone.

They used to leave by the same door they entered.
They used to listen to the gossip of the moon.

They used to bury charms in the lawn
to keep evil out of the house.

But you can't keep evil out. Even red-breasted
robins can tell you that. Or should I say

something more positive? The sun will warm
our bones. Apple trees will bloom

days after the cold has passed.
Robins, I've been told, came to us

from far away, bringing with them songs
we have waited all year to sing.

Mythological

The longest moment lingers
beneath the apple trees in my back lawn
where honeybees get sozzled on blossoms
and stagger as they fly from shadow to light,
from shadow to light, from ecstasy
to euphoria, and back again,
where sunlight dapples and dances
with an unexpected breeze, breaks
over every branch and shatters
in glory upon the ground,
where even gods and goddesses
would come to play
if anyone still allowed them the quiet
comfort of being, allowed them
an unrepentant passion
that everyone could believe, and join in,
and find in their own humdrum lives
and toss-away days, and the longer I wait
here with my lover
like ancient sweethearts
from thousands of years ago,
the longer I can believe
we might be a part of forever,
coming and going and coming and going,
a cluster of stars swirling down upon us
as softly as apple blossom petals
landing upon our unclothed bodies,
in our unkempt hair,
waiting centuries for someone
to tell our story
with one long and lingering breath.

Out of Alignment

—after Matthew Wolfe's multimedia artwork,
Pandemic Evolution-Day 39

From this
river valley in West Virginia,
                    Mercury is a
bottle of black nail polish, ash
                    and cinder
to decorate the body. Venus is
                    a magnifying lens
with a knack for noticing my every flaw.
                    Mars is a pair
of sunglasses, a sister with reflective sight.
                    I cannot see
those cold, red eyes. Jupiter is an empty tumbler
                    with indentations
where someone's burning touch reshaped the glass.
                    Saturn is nothing
but shards and shatters. Uranus is a pot-
                    bellied bud vase
without a flower. And Neptune is a crystal-
                    cut vessel empty
at the dinner table. Dishes and flatware
                    clank and scrape
in the kitchen as I stand outside the window.
                    The sun, my grandmother
told me, can burn me blind if I look
                    directly at it.
As though she knew someone who had.
                    As though
I wouldn't squint and look away.

Tatterdemalion

If there were a way to keep birds out of berry vines,
                    my grandmother knew it,
two posts pushed into the earth, twine stretched
                    between them, old aluminum
pie pans strung so they could chatter with every breeze.
                    Today, a robin preened
and keened in the dogwood as I started the lawn mower.
                    It roared beneath her,
but she didn't flinch or fly. Something tells me
                    nothing will keep her
from the tart green apples that already bend
                    their own branches. The mulberry
tree is stripped clean. I'm not sure the old tricks work
                    anymore, thrashers
and vireos, sparrows and grackles. I could be
                    an apparition here
on the ground where windfalls wither. I could be
                    a child whose father
tunes the television and the radio to two different games,
                    all those voices
a static drifting out windows, haunting the afternoon.
                    I could be the child
standing outside those windows listening to the songs
                    of birds and the strains
of insects. Someone once told me something shiny,
                    something that scatters
sunlight will keep birds from the harvest. But only
                    a straw man can startle a crow.

Zeptosecond

—a trillionth of a billionth of a second, or a decimal point followed by 70 zeroes and a 1. (livescience.com)

Contrary to reason, everything
gets smaller. The house no longer
holds my every breath. My father's soul
shrinks in his body, the last few crumbs
of mercy. It's been reported that time
is shattered further, a glass bottle
broken over and over to dust,
then atoms, then particles of collision
and theory. If I keep dividing the space
between my father and me, I will never arrive.
Maybe I can stretch time the same way
if I experience each moment.
But even a moment is too long. It must be
torn down to its infinitesimal parts,
so I can stay there forever, whatever
that may be. How can the universe keep
expanding, giving us more room
to explore? And tons of dust fall
through the atmosphere to add mass
to the earth, which causes a heaviness
I cannot get out from under. Out from under,
a salamander wriggles from the shadow
of one rock to the shadow of another.
The shadow of my father.
For no reason I can think, I waste
even the smallest pieces of time.

Learning to Fish the Little Kanawha

First, you need a father like mine,
nothing but a pale splinter of flesh
in his work clothes, with skin of glass
from working in the local factory as a gaffer,
a mysterious job pulled up out of the sand
down near the river, the inseam of town.

He will teach you how to make a sieve
out of the finest mesh of screen, so fine
if feels like silk when it's wet. And you won't
understand how he knows which parts of the stream
are loaded with minnows, who taught him this,
or if it's just the fact he's been here all his life.

You will splash through the water,
both of you, until you wear that old calcium
smell that gets trapped under all the limestone
and mudstone. You won't even see anything
moving until he pulls up the net, all that silver
in one pocket, all those strange, vitreous eyes.

Then you're going to need an uncle
so generous he gives everything away
until all he has left is clothes too small
for his belly and a shack in the woods,
though you're not sure exactly where
since you never go visit him anyway.

He's always treading that thin line
between *kind* and *crazy*, and you're not
the only one who thinks so, because
he's spent his whole life telling tall tales
around town, spitting phlegm through his teeth,
pretending someone, anyone, was listening.

He will carry the minnow bucket,
only he will call them *minnies*,
not for what they are, but for their size.
He will set them in the river tied to his ankle
to keep them from drifting off,
the fist-sized lid slack as his mouth, slipping open.

And maybe, just maybe, you'll need a sister,
the only sibling you have, who loves you
so much you almost feel bad about it.
But what can you do? She's the one
who put a hook in your thumb
when she was trying to cast,

but that might have been your fault,
standing where you were, not paying attention.
Oh, and won't you be jealous? Not because
she's a girl, but because she's the only one
of all of you who ever pulled a cat from the water,
and she didn't even know it was on the line.

But what will really get you, I mean
right down to that mysterious empty place inside,
will be the way she reeled it in. Without a fight.
As though it had wanted, all along,
to be led where it could turn
into a man, get up and walk away.

Most of all, you're going to need that boulder
half into the bank and half into the water,
a boulder, to you, the size of the world,
at least on this day, along this little river.
A place where you can watch the twigs
and leaves slide by, and you will see

all the perfect rings where insects touch
the surface. Everyone will be quiet, so quiet
you can hear the river feeling its way
down the banks. No one will say what this is.
You will have to guess when the hook is set
because, in this lifetime, you will never be told.

Living with What I Cannot Find

—after *Red Poppies*, by Mary Cassatt

I can't tell you the pleasures of the world.
That is something you must walk into,
bobbing red heads of flowers,
whispers of yellow, white, and blue,
the lace of green leaves beneath your feet.
Cities grow unseen past the horizon, quick
as an ache. But I can tell you I remember
my mother, my grandmother, my sister
digging for the roots. They wanted
to transplant the beauty of living things,
to spread the paint of one hillside
upon another. But sometimes
beauty does not hold. Soil is not the same
from one plot to another. Listen to me,
speaking of ideals as though everything
is as simple as a dwindling sky, a few
lingering clouds, a modest shadow
on the hill in the distance. I can't tell you
what made me say those things. Maybe
the tall grass behind me says
what I want to hear, tells me
a day like this is all I need.
If you want to find me, you can,
out beyond the edges of this
                    perfect world.

If a Tree Falls in the Forest

It does make a sound, you know. The branches
reach out instinctively to catch the earth.

Leaves wave upward in locks and tresses.
My sister and I leap from the roof

of an unfinished building, the trunks of our bodies
plummeting. Her hair is like that, swept

toward the sky. We love the tickle of gravity
in our stomachs, fledglings ready to fling

ourselves at the world. Our grandmother is a tree,
one of those shade-bearing deciduous trees alone

in a field, carved by lightning. We know
a storm is coming. Clouds gather so thick

they block the sun, wind so fierce it stings
quicker than bees. In some trunks, you can

find honey in hollow spaces. All that buzzing,
louder as you approach. All those birds that go
unmentioned, high among the trembling leaves.

Lynnette, Early Spring, 1979

This is for you, because I never told you
how afraid I was the day our mother left
the house, sure she would never come back.
But that's only part of the fear. The illness
had been left untreated so long

I convinced myself I was going to die.
And what could I do for you then.
You would have been alone, the pretty
little girl who grew up fast taking care
of her father, a Victorian daughter

in high collars and tight buttons,
worried whether meals were too cold
or starchy, if the last few specks of dust
on the bookshelves could wait until tomorrow
to be cast back to the cosmos

with a gentle rubbing. I know
Mom left by the back door to avoid passing
my room, not wanting me to see
how weak she could become. And what if
I had wasted time wondering

what moved the shadows, the barest light
frisking windows like a woman's hands
sopping her hot child's head. It was then
my visions began. Still I have them,
false birds in a hazy sky, austere

people stepping in and out of walls,
the rumbling mass of roaches and spiders,
imps that waver in public spaces
waiting for me to shout their names.
It is like this. But maybe you can

only understand fear as a dirt road
late at night when the trees huddle close
as ogres, and the stars open their tiny mouths
to call out their warnings. Warnings
you will never hear. Thunder of a wild bird

scared to flight. Stifle of leaves behind you.
Do you understand now? Do you see
what became of me back then, all that time
alone, counting the metal sufferings of doorlatches
again and again, listening to the world

break as easily as glass in a storm door?
I couldn't even lift my head off the pillow,
my brain nothing but a lead weight,
the kind of thing our father once said
farmers would use to drown a sackful

of unwanted cats. This became the stuff
of our nightmares in the age of divorce.
You were the last person on earth
when everyone else had departed for Mars
or Jupiter or the moon. Once they broke

the atmosphere of my breath, it didn't matter
where they were going. They were just gone.
Today I thought of this while I was planting
the peppers a neighbor gave me two days ago.
Dirt under my nails, I entered the house

of my healing, the place of my superstitions.
Remember, we swore never to believe
what our parents believed. When you come,
you cannot stay long. Leave by the same door
in which you entered. Anything could happen.

Contrapuntal

They are there,
those little black apostrophes of spring.
Your sister kneels to look at them,
or perhaps your brother, or cousin,
or anyone, but someone, always someone,
because this is one of those
great discoveries of childhood—*duality*—
that goes beyond the bipolar world

and into the next.
Then it is your turn to knee the cracked earth
in that posture of holding
because all the wriggling creatures below you
have two names, silly names—
tadpole, pollywog—they both make you laugh,
your head filling
with that sensation,

like hydrogen, helium, argon,
all the loose elements of the world, unseen,
you don't even know you are touching
even when they slide across your palm.
Some of the tiny pre-frogs
scan the surface of the puddle for air
upside down, intestines showing
in their glassy bellies like thumbprints,

the kind left on handicrafts or pottery,
that one swirl of proof that, yes,
this was touched by the creator,
no matter how human that might be.
And this place is drying up.
You can't help but wonder
how terrible frogs are at parenting—
they must know how many will die.

That must be part of the secret,
the double, the duo, the twin, a Gemini
sacrifice, the living and dying
and everything that happens in between,
the constellations of memory,
that one small piece of the brain that can never be
cut out and destroyed, not even by aluminum
and psychoactive drugs. We tell ourselves

this is nature, this is what it's all about,
condemning ourselves for the desire to think
otherwise. Nearby, the stream is shrinking
to thread and twine, smelling of its own
struggle, that cold mud, minnowy smell
lingering beneath the water oak and beech.
Right here, by this puddle,
this simple, self-destructive world—

we wait impatiently
for something to happen, hoping the steps of evolution,
metamorphosis, come fast, pushing out
the legs and webbed feet, taking all of the tail
into the body, like us, *human,*
having escaped what we could of our primordial
beginnings. We see there is
more than one way to escape,

more than one way to leave the old self
behind, and not so much becoming
as refining ourselves to live as best we can
in our cramped and quartered spaces.
We must know we can never be these people
again, we must know that we will stand
and grow the slightest bit upward with our mouths
curved and lapping at the immense parallel sky.

Associative

Every little thing has its own
memory of pain, the long fibers of the body
imprinting whatever comes close
by the ruin it will cause.

It is a hidden evolutionary pocket
within each person. In some it is a dark
spot on the lung, or a lesion
on the stomach. And in others,

a reddish sore
in the lining of the throat, a subtle misfire
through the coral recesses of the brain,
or a mass of snakes

rippling through the skull.
Things link automatically, candles
and fingernails, the night the electricity
went out, and your father

decided with the flicker
of the taper that the infection was too much
and pulled the calcium shell away
from your clam-wrinkled nail bed.

Or with pliers the afternoon
he yanked a bloody cactus thorn
out of your thumb. And you think
you can never forgive him

for the things he had to do.
Then there is the way you walk,
club-footed as though you were twelve
and still limping with the honeybee

sting that swelled your leg
to twice its size. Or weak-thighed
where the wasp left a scar
while you waited for the school bus

in a rickety, wooden shelter
where someone else had drawn
Neolithic images of men with giant pricks
and women with back-breaking tits.

And no matter how long you live,
you will never forget this, how insignificant
you felt among those impossible icons,
cultural gods and goddesses,

beings that could never exist.
And, at this point, you might even remember
someone else's pain, possibly the woman
next door who can't even look

at a deck of cards
because her husband used poker
as an excuse to go out and screw around.
Possibly the heavy man across the street

who mows his lawn every two days.
You can see it festering in the flab
of his chest and bulk of his stomach,
the way he cares too much

about his gay son
and prostitute daughter.
You can see it in the dandelions
banished to the fence line,

and the way he hates us all
for letting them bloom like blisters
in our own yards so that he has to fight
the wind-blown seeds.

Perhaps everyone here
is a prodigy, all of us with an innate
talent for magnifying the things
that hurt us most.

We are everyday virtuosos,
small and brilliant as sparrows,
singing the dangers of the world,
diving in and suffering it out.

Expulsion

Gardens hush with evening,
foliage strapped with darkness
and the sort of quiet that speaks
with other voices—strong, clear,
passionate voices—the only song of night
we will ever know. We are surprised
that something has waited all day
to compose this nocturne.
Caddisflies, springtails, assassin bugs.
We don't even know the bodies
out there, like ghosts
pulled up from wet grasses.
We cannot decipher the messages
clattering one over the other to reach us
as we sleep. Blister beetles,
checkerspots, and mourning cloaks.
They carve their disenchantment
even over a world of our own creation—
the brazen drone of street lights,
the hum of car engines three streets over,
the bombast of town after town
filling every valley, every copse,
every riverbed and flood plain, moving
through each tributary, ridge and rock.
Ichneumons, earwigs, hawkmoths.
We hear the brief joining of short lives.
We hear anxiety rubbing out of every wing,
every leg, and every mandible.
Each life is so common to its place, its time,
its inherent and unpreventable behavior.
Carrion beetles, army worms, and walking sticks.
By morning, a shred of moon
clings like lint to the hem of the sky.
Again, we are sure that someone lay in our beds

beside us while we preoccupied ourselves
with one breath and another,
someone who would take us as we are,
never asking whether or not we were ready to go.

Continuity

The last paper wasp
of the season gets trapped
between the rain-streaked window
and the dusty mesh of the screen.
Something I never would have noticed
all summer, same as the parking lot
attendant dehydrating in his enclosure.
Or the top-rated FM DJ, talking
to no one in particular all afternoon.
Or the electrician dying with a rare bone
cancer. Or the post office custodian
who served in Europe during World War
Two, who never touched a whore
and never killed a man. Or the quilter
with stitches for vertebrae and thimbles
for fingerprints. Or the portrait painter,
the oldest living woman I may ever know.
Normally, who would have noticed
the girl with the grim reaper ankle tattoo?
Or the Catholic boy's wife teaching
physics in Columbus, Ohio?
Then there are the strangers.
Like the middle-aged waitress drunk
and being eaten out at the bar
with five men watching from their booths.
Like the housewife with MS who takes
a beating, forgiveness for apologies
and one more diamond ring. Like
the gay man pretending to be a father
to a five-year-old girl, because
it's easier for him, because its easier
for everyone. It doesn't matter.
We enter autumn hesitant as bees,
or slugs waiting for the last cool fog

to call up desire, the slick knots
of perpetuation. Some of us hate to see
the leaves turn so fast. Some us enjoy
the color. Whoever we are, whatever we do,
we tend to our work, the spoonful
of good we pull from our bodies
replenishing each other, every day.

On the Occasion of Solemnity
—after Andrew Wyeth's *Study for the Bachelor*

Try to see what I see. First,
there must be sunlight.
Not just any sunlight,
but the kind that is only seen
pouring over your shoulder.

And it has to be enough
to dry the cloth, specifically,
the single white shirt
hanging on the line
strung across the porch.

And the shirt must hang
upside-down, fixed there
by three clothespins.
It will appear to be tortured,
those two loose arms

giving in to the loneliness
swept in on an afternoon
breeze. The scrollwork
that frames the porch
speaks a soliloquy

of someone who tastes
the bitterness of time,
who licks the crumbs
from his lips. The wash pan
is the only imperative

waiting below the shirt
to catch its gray shadow
and try to make it as white
as the cuffs and the collar,
the buttonholes and seams.

At the other corner,
a twig of philosophy grows
up behind a leaning board.
No. That's not right.
A twig of forsythia

just touches the light.
You will not see a shadow
loosed from this greenery.
All of its substance,
all of its meaning stays there

in those leaves. And
is that a cat? Or is it
a black smudge with eyes?
Is it a small universe
with two as yet unnamed stars?

I can't tell you.
You must determine which of these
drab colors are real,
and which are the flotsam and jetsam
of the life before us.

The weeds must be growing
through the slats of the porch,
and they must go to seed
on their weak stems
in the heat of every summer.

A few loose bits of shade hang down
like ripped fabric from the slats.
They must be there
or the rest of the world
would not make sense.

I'm sorry. I mean the world
will never make sense.
I've been possessed by a strange solitude.
Look further.
Behind the shirt you will see

a demon hiding
where you would imagine
in the brushstrokes of darkness.
He comes to visit
when you least expect.

Give him room.
Let him breathe
the uncertainty of the air.
Let him pull on
your clean, white shirt.

The Plight of Frankenstein's Monster

How it was done, I can't say,
the top of the head cut loose,
the brain of someone forgotten

attached and articulated
with each sensitive nerve.
Is it any wonder

I've always felt out of place?
Perhaps I suffer a medical
disorder, or a crisis of identity,

my inner self incompatible
with my outward appearance.
Who is it? Who stitched

these fingertips into their whorls
and loops? I don't know how,
but someone picked up every bone

and glued them together with flayed
portions of muscle. The organs
keep shifting, unsure in their places,

afraid of rejection.
My sex is foreign, my skin a patchwork
of cells and dust. What is the thread

that holds me together?
Will these wounds ever heal?
Are there any balms or tinctures,

any ointments or salves to soothe
my frayed edges? All these parts,
I can only call them ancestors.

These eyes are my grandfathers.
This tongue, a grandmother
I never knew.

The Zombie

Death cannot touch me anymore.
Starlight and moonlight hold no sway
over my emotions. Not even a rainstorm
passing over at 6:52 can make me pray

to any neutered gods. The sky keeps yelling,
a thunderous voice. My aimless bones
are able to amble through graveyards,
scuffle through streets.

My thoughtless and shriveled brain has only
interstellar radiation to thank, or voodoo curse,
or demonic plague. It doesn't matter.
Emergency sirens answer thunder

with panic. I can feel my arteries collapse,
my lungs and heart interred in the clutch of my chest.
The first dead man I saw was my grandfather,
an atheist wrapped in the trappings of religion.

I stood by the pale, prone body in his widower's black,
sunlight through stained glass, a parade of sorrow.
I expected him to get up and walk away, loosen his tie,
unbutton his cuffs, start a new life

in some other godforsaken town. And here
I am on the verge of something supernatural,
all hatred, and necromancy, and desires of the flesh,
because flesh is all I am. The earth keeps trying

to hold me down, dirt and stone
clinging to my shoes and sleeves,
dropping into the corners of the kitchen
and the bedroom, dust in my eyes,

ashes in my hair. I would wander this world,
but what's the use? All that can be found is buildings,
and trees, and sky, and leaves, and people
screaming to be saved, to be bathed in the light.

2

~ Swarms of unanswered prayers ~

Elliptical Orbit

Some people count the days. Hundreds of them
disappear, the planet revolving and spinning

off into the universe, taking me and everything I own with it.
You, too, I suppose.

     We are always in revolution,
taking up a cause, marching in the streets, marching in the rain,

but today is all sunshine and apple blossoms.
Given another hundred days, perhaps

I can reach up into the trees, leaves quivering around my hands.
Perhaps I can pluck tart fruit from a high branch and bring it

to my mouth. Perhaps I can bite the unwashed flesh and taste
every second it took to get here, this moment, this interlude

suspended above with seeds that arrive grateful but shaken.
Grateful but shaken,

     the world a rare and ripening yield,
I am unsure of my place on the calendar, my place

on the timeline from Big Bang to Big Crunch.
There are only so many days.

     This day breathes
under birds and blooms, under breeze and trees,

under wisp and whisper. Wake up. The world is in light,
in darkness   in light   in light.

After the Storm

Limbs down, unripe apples spoiled across the lawn,
I wonder if I have angered some unseen entity.

Have I been dismissed from paradise?
Am I being punished for an offense I committed

unknowingly? Was I warned? Was I forbidden
but one thing? I planted these trees

under a susurration of starlings, under a vernal and vacuous sky.
I should be the one to make music for this garden,

adding birds and bugs to voice long afternoons of passion,
to celebrate morning exclamations of joy.

Night should come with its own song,
a shiver of wind under leaves, a shushing of rain on the roof.

But I have no control over the weather.
I have no say about serendipity,

the slapdash ways of the world, and gods.
There, I've said it. I've conceded to the almighties,

who delight in punishment, who take
pleasure from the suffering of others.

Perhaps it is just chance that broke these trees.
At least then I could refute supernatural control.

I could disregard swarms of unanswered prayers
buzzing around as though they were bees

and my ears were blossoms of hope,
whatever that may be.

Cruelty can be chalked up to coincidence,
which is not a god, but a fickle cousin to fate.

How do I make sense of this entropy?
How can I believe the branches I climb can hold me

when my body was built for an endless, ungraceful fall?

Four Years After Surgery

I can stand. I can walk and move and turn around
      to see what I must leave behind.
My spine is a stack of dishes, a balancing act,
      a clattering of ceramic that keeps me
upright. Each night, I climb the ladder,
      each loose rung. If you look closely,
you may see a scar, a vertical scratch,
      a faint reminder that we could all be
paralyzed. One piece could crumble,
      and every bridge spanning the world
could moan and twist and fall. Every skyscraper
      could collapse floor by floor into the streets
below, the byways below, the hell below.

I can stand. I can raise my fists and pound my feet.
      There is a piece of metal in my back,
the beams and bolts that hold the world together,
      a country, a continent, a plate that shifts
and causes earthquakes. Even the rings of trees
      can be compromised, can be worn away
by beetles and birds, can be torn from the earth
      by a brutal wind. Let the miracle begin.
Let the spine stand tall, unfurl with apple blossoms,
      grow rich with forbidden fruit. Let me get
to my feet to march through daylight and night.
      Let me be stronger than the straw I carry.

Waiting for the Coming Storm

There will be some pain.
For me, a demon in the lower back,
a jab and a pinch, the body's prophecy.

My grandmother has needles in her hands,
                        and I'm not surprised.
Most of her life has been scissors and thread.

There will be a change in the light,
a body rushing between the sun and home.
A giant bird, perhaps; a cryptid, maybe.

I have come to the age where I feel the blur of seasons,
that indefinite sway of sadness and otherwise.
A certain weight in the atmosphere

pushes down upon my roof and makes these walls
creak and moan, an ocean of pressure
begging to be let in. But I will not let it in.

My sister's knees, my mother's teeth, my father's heart—
all of us have our warnings. Even my lover complains
about the weather. My grandmother says I must learn

                    the song of the rain crow,
turn my back to the wind, like leaves. She says
I must never look into the eyes of the monster

that drags thunder on its wings,
for I would surely live with lightning,
a demon that dances up and down the spine.

A Prediction of Rain

The neighbor's peonies lower
their giant heads, paint the ground below
with heavy thoughts.

And, just like that,
I've made the flowers a symbol
of self, given them emotions

without knowing what they feel.
I don't even know the neighbors—
the man, the woman, the boy

who will surely be grown
before he realizes it.
Iris blossoms wither

like old men and are gone
too soon, which just goes to show
I'm pondering the inevitable.

And I don't know if I can handle that.
This afternoon, I watch a robin
gather grasses along the fence.

It must be time for a second brood.
I hope the first didn't succumb
to the cold snap,

though that would explain
the sadness, these perennials still here
after a season of loss,

all this attempt at beauty
while the mourning dove sings.
Day or night, I never see

the family next door,
but I know they are there
by the position of cars

in their driveway, by the lawn
freshly mowed. Or is it mown,
which sounds like suffering?

Architecture for Elephants

What I imagine is a monsoon,
tree limbs as rafters, green leaves as shingles,

a herd of elephants gathered below
while the weather whips and tosses the world.

But I don't live where behemoths roam,
crash through the house when I'm trying to sleep.

All I know of pachyderm behavior
comes from zoo enclosures and nature shows,

how they rub their hides against
whatever will take their weight, how they express

joy in pools of water, how they nuzzle
their young with those expressive trunks. In some parts

of the world, people build abstract
structures to share space with tuskers, to watch them

from mammoth observation platforms.
Ancient Romans carved these colossal creatures in relief

on marble panels—stone wrinkles,
stone eyes, stone blankets draped over

stone backs. I don't want to mention
poachers, destruction of habitat, and all the atrocities

that come naturally to others
of my kind. *Kind*, meaning likeness,

not tenderness or beneficence.
For that, you need to witness an elephant caress

the bones of loved ones long-dead
under the shelter of trees, trees reaching up into the rain.

Barometer

Water, this time,
right up to the front steps,
the stream knotting itself
into uncontrollable spasms.
This is the first time
it has ever come this far,

the water table arguing
its limits with pepper grass
and ragwort, laughing
against the buckeye and the maple.
And it never seems to stop,
this rain coming down heavy

as sugar, melting
to brown, caramel twists
that disappear through the culvert
where one summer my sister found
the skull of a horse, the implosion
of those two, huge empty eye sockets

sifting runnels and trickles
of red clay mud. The salamander
that crawled the cavern
of bone where the brain had been.
The pebbles panned into a new medulla
like broken chips of thought.

We were afraid to cross under
that dark bridge, the bones,
the spider webs, the sickly weeds
that grappled through the stones
toward thin summer rods of light.
The long tunnel of our lives.

And then crossing
the neighbor's ten acres of yard
to get to the green swill
of the swimming hole where we learned
to dive, learned to use our hands
to keep us from death,

placing them side by side
in one flat plank before our bodies.
Then the rumble of liquid in our ears
and the reaching, the turning
for the surface as though
we were being born again and again.

All around, the air is muggy
with cloud sweat. Unnamable finches
jump at the closed pods of dandelion
seedheads, and twitch the rain
off their mottled backs. This morning the sky
purples with electricity. Later,

we will hear the flash flood stories
of picture frames and mattresses,
everything covered in a silt so fine
that it gets into the skin of things.
A cloud so dark
we should have seen it coming.

(Omen) The Neighborhood of Make-Believe

A bird sings in the rain
in the middle of the night,
which ancestors tell us is a sign

of something more mysterious.
Something more mysterious

happens in our neighbor's homes,
makes us whisper about the young
man who killed himself,

or the couple screaming at
each other in the darkest hours.

In the darkest hours, there
should be owl and nightjar,
mockingbird and killdeer

calling out in our dreams.
In our dreams, wind hushes

through trees, waves shush
against shore, and someone stays
up all night with someone else.

Someone else is rushed away
with sirens and lights, people

at their windows stoking
the worst fears. The worst
fears lie in wait for me

to turn off the light, so they can
stretch out through the house,

fill every shadow. Every shadow
has a source, a body it mimics,
a body that throws it away,

a sense of self cast upon the earth.
Cast upon the earth, every atom

of water moves toward the lowest
elevation, unless it is trapped.
Unless it is trapped, air moves

as though it has a purpose, and
a bird sings in the rain.

Unmoored

Quiet street, my river,
my tributary to there
and where, takes me unaware
today. How did sunlight find
its way here? I'm beginning
to question my place
in the world, gray water
still as pebbles,
stagnant, people trapped
in the corner of my eye,
floaters that won't blink
away. Everyone I know.

Everyone I know is adrift
on other rivers. Elm Street,
Oak Street, Division Street,
a place that keeps us
apart. First, Seventh, Tenth
and a Half, all add to an ocean
I've never seen. Those who have
never return. The water there
is vast and alters perception.

Did you know when you drink
sea water, salt dehydrates
your body, your thirst
unbearable? I trust those who say
there is a current that runs
swift beneath the surface,

creatures that wait in muck
and roots, among twigs and rocks.
Remember, salvation flows
from where to there, at first
towards us, then away.

The Size of Myth

The hospital where my grandmother died
collects sunsets and zephyrs across town.
The Ohio River runs mindless as Lethe nearby.

I know someone who fell
from the bridge. He plunged
into that hopeless channel

where catfish grow the size of cars.
I know someone who lost control,
drove down the banks, barely made it out alive.

West winds wear a path
through town. People start to feel safe,
despite the threat of a storm that lags behind.

Survival is a matter of calculation.
One summer, a barge loaded with fireworks
exploded. People leapt off the deck

into their mirror images, ripples
and flames, an unholy flower blooming
in darkness, completed only by its own reflection.

Downriver, a chemical plant radiates
night with sodium light, as though something alien
landed in a field, how it makes a flowing

river glow. My grandmother used to call a breeze
a promise. I've been known to watch it dance
on the surface of deeper waters.

August Everywhere

I remember my grandfather saying,
It is August everywhere, and me
thinking he meant everything in the world
was this confrontation of land and sea,
everything was North Carolina in summer,
sunlight piecing together in the east
to make a hot ball of flame
above the earth.

But now, I think he meant the crows,
how they were the only constant, sitting in trees
and fields wherever there was death.

He loved the salt water more than anything,
waited for it to boil up to his feet and pull
the ground out from under him, for the ocean
to reach up with broken waves,
pulling itself up past the rocks and catching
the roots of grasses, dragging up like some giant
miscreant to stand and walk and breathe again.

He was sure that change meant life,
that some things were meant to be pulled
far out to sea to fight for air.

Diurnal

The heavy boots of night walk off.
Like someone not ready to go, must go.
The woman who makes a game
of this leaving, for her children,
for herself, to believe this is not
how it always ends—the drunk man
shouting at an empty house,
breaking anything she might have
left behind, the many things
that change, the aberration
of footstep after footstep
trailing across the lawn.

Perhaps it is the insanity
of a man who loses his son,
his daughter, and his father
to the rain, the hard slaps of flood.
The way he dives into the stream,
the unexpected grab and claw,
the grappling of his shoes.
And the search team, later,
bringing back every body but his,
giving up as though he never existed
and never would.

Or the girl who waits
with covers knotted up to her face,
and the steady tapping of the second hand
on a clock five minutes fast.
Then the rhythm of feet approaching
from down the hall where her mother
fakes sleep. Her father undoes the sheets.
He doesn't tell her to be quiet anymore.
This has gone on so long.
Some things go simply unsaid.

You forget and you forget.
You tell yourself such fantasies.
You suddenly believe there are gods and goddesses
who chase each other across the sky,
who care for their human progeny
in unhuman ways.
You fall into yourself. Kick your feet
in spirals. Call yourself by secret names.
You find the world beneath you,
sorry that it must be there.

Day is another drapery,
a cloth over the window
saturated with dust. It is the hand
that pulls the curtain aside
so that more can be seen.
It is the release,
and all the loose particles
bright for a moment.
Before evening, the sound of someone
walking. Closer. Then closer.

Round Trip

Waves against the pilings,
I boarded the ferry to Staten Island.
I wasn't going anywhere,

only passing by. My friend told me
it was the best way to see her,

Lady Liberty on an overcast afternoon.
I thought I could fall in love
under those clouds, the scribbled

silhouettes of seagulls overhead.
The vessel rocked a little

while wind clung to the railing,
while I watched my friend struggle
to light a cigarette. It's been so long ago,

all the details create their own fog.
I think there was light climbing

the statue, highlighting
shadows in folds of sculpture.
What we talked about, I don't remember,

but I'd never felt more like a tourist
or an immigrant, in awe of a symbol

of hope. We debarked, walked around
the empty port, reboarded for the trip back
where we disappeared

among the architecture, surrounded,
as we were, by water.

Early Spring Disciples

Sun finds its way around
edges of cloud drift,
the kind of clouds that show
their heaven and their heartache.

When day hits the pool,
water furrows. Children dangle
their feet at the edge,
dream of walking

across the surface.
I know this dream.
But the temperature is not quite
right, hovers near the cool side

of warm. The season is still
pulling on its robes.
Even afternoon light
sinks to the bottom,

swims and shimmers,
glimmers, shines.

Humidity

The atmosphere is bohemian.
Wind drags itself through
tresses of numberless trees.

Mulberry shivers at the touch.
It's one of those days
when the sun explodes,

and the earth perspires
with an untamed love.

Monarda flares in the field.
Butterfly weed trembles by the road.
Grasses along the chain link fence
weave their way upward.

Even water on a day like today
rises. Everyone strips off their clothing, all
whisked away with a sultry touch.

Paradise has its limits,
but what those are may never be known.

It is the way of bees to gather in hives,
cool themselves with rapturous wings.

In the full light of afternoon,
even the breeze steals a breath.

Standing still is not an option.
Waterfalls thin to slow ecstasy.
And the naked world cries out with joy.

Each second belongs to the passion of another.
If I find my way home,

there will be no sleep.
Tangle my wicked body with dreams.

Narcissism

Caught by this river,
        I lean out. I think
of my lover drowning.
          How deeply must I plummet
to find bottom, twig
        and leaf, rock and mud?

———

My face is in the water.
        There must be a breeze
that ripples fear. I think
        of my lover drowning.
Upriver, a bridge
        mocks its own reflection.

———

How many of us have
        fallen or leaped? Even
the swirl and flow
        has no memory. And I think
of my lover drowning.
        I, too,

———

have had fluid fill my lungs.
        Somehow, I broke
the surface. People ask
        how I can love the water
this much. I tell them

———

this is the last place
                I was alive. I think
of my lover drowning.
                Downstream, an island
pushes against the flow.
                Tree roots claw

———

at whatever might save them.
                I've seen the struggle
of savior and sacrifice.
                I've seen them go under
until it was impossible
                to return. I think

———

of holding my lover,
                water still dripping
from his brow, across
                his face.

Mid-Season in Zone 6

There's simply no use trying
to grow a garden here. Not the way tomato
vines relax in the summer heat
and rot with each heavy rain.

Not the way corn stalks
lay flat with another hard wind,
or the way cucumber vines wilt in this
humidity. Down in the soil

the carrots grow fat and pithy,
come up with a rotten taste. And radishes
gone to seed split their sides
as though the bright skins

cannot hold all that blistering, white flesh.
All the while the half-turned
pumpkins twist off their stems
and go pale against the earth.

This ground is haunted
with aggies and green plastic
soldiers, the remnants of an old school yard
turned up beside stones

by the tiller's blades,
the machine that kicks and grabs
at soil as though searching
for these things. On the other side

of the yard is a sidewalk
that begins at the road and ends
with untrimmed June grass,
the lapse of a hundred feet.

I have never seen a picture
of the school, surely wood and rotting
even when my grandfather gazed
at oil-slicked paper panes

that must have one night
caught fire and glowed in this valley,
hot and bright as the balled fist
of the sun punching its way up

from the ridge. And so,
abandonment, these toys
only allow themselves
to resurface a few every year.

They are tiny, whispered
secrets of children, the only things
that persist, like multiflora rose
brambling through horse pastures,

choking off the chance
for anything else to grow.
And yet here is the cauliflower,
a huge white brain

continuing its dreams. Here
is the holy cabbage, folding hand
over hand in prayer that this year
there will be enough to feed us all.

3

~ Replace my heart with an apple ~

Revolution

I inaugurate spring with the first cutting of the lawn.
The air is still hard with defeat,
and the garden languishes last season's struggle
with drought and ravenous beetles.

But today there are fists on every tree,
the blossoming knuckles of the apple
ready themselves for the fight to come,
and the dogwood clenches every bud

knowing there will be blood. Even the sun has itself
all balled up with frustration. I can feel its anger
battering the world, mourning
the good sense God gave a goose.

I have never seen war, but I can tell what it does
to bodies and minds and spirits, ghosts who wander the earth
seeking vengeance and justice
and other things no one ever seems able to find.

Daffodils already bow low,
their stunning faces cast down in shame
because they've done nothing; nothing, that is,
but the practice of being shameful.

I find the first butterfly of the season frantic in the shed,
nervous as a refugee stepping into the light.

Forgive me if I march against the wind.
Eventually, my hands will open,
the petals unfurl.
And isn't that astonishing?

The Nubbins

I pull pips off of my apple trees.
I remove those tough, useless expectations
that sucker the one true apple on the branch.

Yes, I know pips is not the right word,
but it's the one that seems to fit
for the way I bend stems until they snap and fall,
the way they hide in the grasses below.

I cast off this undeveloped fruit
in hopes that what I leave will be better,
larger, sweeter, more ripe under the sway of the sun.

So much waste, so much potential is thrown to shadow
and shrift, which is a kind of confession.

Perhaps this is what I do as I push into the branches,
shriving to robins that complain at my presence,
shrill at my movement through the leaves.

Who can claim these trees? Who can claim
the bounty promised here? Rain crows mourn
in spiritual tones. I cannot reach the highest clutches
where bloom is rewarded with flesh and seed.

Last night's rain still beads upon this morning's stillness.
Heavy rainfall is expected again tonight.

Clouds already gather in a coven overhead,
and I know I've changed the meaning of another word.
We will all wish for rain during the dry days of August,
the irresistible knowledge it always brings.

Eve's Theme

Rumor suggests that the names of things originated with me,
even those distinct variations of rain.

But this is not exactly the truth.
Even the smallest creature, the least observed plant,

the most distant star has a voice and speaks
its own appellation. I'm sorry

if you don't understand.
If you are still enough, long enough, you can hear

all those who speak. And as for the gossip of temptation,
don't be so quick to judge.

Even the seeds inside the fruit call out.
                              I listen.

They say bite into the flesh,
let them see the light.

Ontological

Replace my heart with an apple.
Emotional intelligence is hard to come by.
Give it a glossy red skin, tart and sweet flesh,
                              arsenic in every seed.

Exchange my viscera with miles of rope,
knotted and twisted to fill the emptiness
I've come to expect will always be there.

Fill my head with coils and clutches of cobwebs.
The spiders have all moved on
to brighter corners in far less trafficked rooms.

Perhaps I will remember last Tuesday,
or some hazy conversation that meant more
                              all those years ago
than it ever could today.

I don't know who I am, but to be fair,
I don't know you, either.

Strip away my sinew and cartilage.
Sever each muscle. Dry them in the sunlight,
and leave them for eagles to feast.

This has nothing to do with fire, or punishment,
                              or goddesses or gods.

Give me tendrils of morning glory
and trumpet vine and wisteria. Let them cling
together around my bones, which now are oaken
                              branches, hickory twigs.

Take my eyes, and stuff the sockets
with pomegranate seeds, and, yes,
                    I know the mythology,
but I will not give up my blood.
I will not live in darkness.

I will not be dragged away from the fire of stars
                    burning day and night.

Replace my heart with an apple.
Let the knowledge of my freedom clear the sky,
warm the soil, take root, and make a home
where even lesser gods and devils are welcome.

Ascension

I never mow the lawn on Sunday,
   which is how I keep the Sabbath holy.

I am no man of God, and I could never be
   a god among men. When the world ends,

it will be in lightning.
   Electricity will charge the air,

causing hair to stand on end,
   causing lights to flicker and sizzle,

causing sky to shatter and fall.
   People will run for shelter

finally believing in their own
   or someone else's gods because

punishment is the mark of the almighty.
   But today is Sunday,

and a hot breeze sweeps in
   as a reminder that the earth still spins

and holds my body close, a child
   of sod and flame and wind and rain.

So arises a belief in the afterlife.
   Because this life is just not enough.

And, really, it isn't. Something irrational
   overtakes me, fills my heart, and rushes

through my body. I have no control.
    I feel that I could step out

into the untouched grass, I could leap
    toward the sky. I could make my way

into the heavens.
    I tell you, I could.

Provenance

Everything begins here. And by here,
I mean this house, my house.

And to be precise, I mean the kitchen
where the morning sun rouses from the floor.

And to be perfectly honest, I mean the faucet
where cool drops of water leave calcium

residue on the spigot, where centuries pass,
and cave formations care nothing for time,

which comes from a distant source, a waterfall
on an earth-like planet scarred

with ancient wounds. And by wounds,
I mean every love you've ever lost.

And by lost, I mean a quiet room
that no one visits,

a stir of dust motes through fingers of light,
a clock on the wall stopped at 4:16,

regardless of what you think you know.
But to be clear, air thins

the further it reaches
toward the stars. To be understood,

we should walk out of here, walk
into the streets and into the fields.

We should reach up to the heavens.
And by heavens, I mean home.

Hyperbole

By always, I mean intermittent
but ongoing. I mean the hours of sunlight
and minutes that walk through the night.

So when I say I drive through town every day,
you understand
this is not a constant.

Cracks in pavement widen, even
if only by perception. Rainwater fills gaps,
and wind dries the roadway.

Birds, maybe
wrens or finches, peck at sidewalks,
choose the right pebbles

to fulfill their lives. Black cats are everywhere,
but they don't always cross my path.
And when I say everywhere, I mean nothing

more than the fact that black cats are the ones
I notice, and they come
with their own superstitions.

Seasons come and go.
They are downtown employees
waiting for traffic to let up, the lights

to change, the concrete to push them
on their way. So I drive through town
every day. And when I say every day…

well, you know what I mean.
This is home. This is the pattern of wake
and sleep and work and play.

This is the same old sun and clouds and rain
listing god-like above us
since the beginning of time.

In Decline

A couple of lanky teens shoot
                   hoops in the fine mist
of a cloudy afternoon. It's winter
                   but warm, and there
are three small children plotting
                   world domination
in the volleyball sand court,
                   perfect for building
castles and tearing them down.
                   I drive past the park,
wipers on intermittent, the way ahead
                   clear for a moment.
Fractal treetops cut the gray
                   sky, reach out
to tear their way through to the sun
                   we all know is there,
burning off all that furious light.
                   Let them take over,
those pigeons gathered above us on wires,
                   making themselves
symbolic. The number of birds seems
                   to dwindle daily.
I've let grasses and wild
                   flowers go to seed
along the backyard fence where
                   occasionally I find
a feather, and spiderwebs
                   sometimes covered
with dew, and, finally, frost.

Blight

This city does nothing but sleep.
It snoozes, slumbers and snores.

2:15 a.m. comes and goes and leaves
five minutes of rain in the driveway.

Quiet spreads a blanket and turns
off the stars. The moon is new,

and it knows the irony. Streetlights
barely notice how dark the world gets

around them. It's too early for crickets,
and spring peepers have forgotten

the words to this song. The streets
begin to fall apart, chunks of pavement

come to rest, come to rest, come to rest.
I'm sorry, I was dreaming.

I was dreaming of downtown
where sidewalks wither.

I was dreaming of abandoned buildings
staring blindly out over the river,

the river, the lonely river.
If I should die before I wake,

who would notice? Not
the woodbine drowsing

on the backyard fence. Not brick walls
that sleepwalk in the smallest hours of night.

Not thousands of weary people yet to open
their thousands of weary eyes.

Not a Sonnet

—no thanks to Shakespeare

My lover's eyes are nothing like what you're thinking,
and when I use the word *my*, I don't mean to denote
ownership or dominion. I intend a certain intimacy—
sitting at dinner, our knees touching—or later, asleep,
our arms, our hips, our hands fallen where they may.
May what, I couldn't say. And when I say lover,
I don't mean to imply a strictly physical relationship,
a constant passion ravaging the body. We walk
along grocery aisles comparing prices. We sing
and talk and answer tv gameshow questions. Yes,

I said *ravaging*. Sometimes passion shakes your bones
brittle, deprives the body of oxygen, snaps the junctions
in the brain. My lover's temperament is earthquake
and typhoon, tornado and lightning. I wouldn't have it
any other way. And when I drown in the deepest
oceanic trench or suffocate in the exosphere, my lover
is my metamorphosis pulling me back to land, restarting
my heart, blessing air back into my eager, ravaged lungs.

Compensatory

Every summer for five years
we hear reports of the Sunnyside rapist,
of carefree college girls getting caught
in parking garages and side streets.

We suspect everyone.
I even start to wonder about that
homeless man who lays it on thick,
going through his spiel where he played

with BB King in Boston, and all the greats
I've never heard of. But I want to believe
it's true. And so I believe. Even the story
of his wife and kids, working his way back

to Texas or Minnesota or whatever place
he mumbles and calls home, a shadow
in one hand and a beer in the other.
And there on the sidewalk, waiting for the heat

to let up, I empty my pockets
and hand over everything, the quarters,
dimes and nickels, the stray button, the dry cleaning
stub, the hasty notes to myself I will never read

anyway. We stand there like two phantoms
on the verge of dispersion, buying and selling
bits of our lives to see the fog breathe heavy
into the trees. I start thinking of the specters

of all those best friends I left somewhere
in the ditches and gullies of the past,
how they must still be alive,
and how easy it is for me

to live without them. Including the girl
I took downstate for an abortion,
the day of the first snowfall that amounted
to much of anything. She kept asking me

if it was a sign, and I kept saying no.
But that was for her because I couldn't help
but read it as a portent, not a judgment,
as anyone might expect, a catalyst for change.

Even the way she wasn't allowed to eat
all day. I tried to fast with her
and failed, and excused myself because it wasn't
my child, it wasn't my fault, it had nothing

to do with me. I was wrong.
Now, I recognize that ghost for salvation,
like dogs down the block that draw my attention
from the man who keeps asking

for spare change, and acquires, instead,
the smallest of my secrets. I kick
at a pigeon that has been pecking at pebbles,
like any other stupid bird, for its survival.

Years later, I know they will apprehend
the rapist, an associate professor of engineering,
I think. Or something we condition ourselves
to take on faith as normal. They must have trapped him

through his DNA, since he always wore a mask.
I didn't read the article all that closely.
But by the time this gets out, it isn't much more than fodder
for darkness, the odd corners and seams

where we lose ourselves one small portion at a time,
digging up handful after handful we think nothing of giving away.

The Boy in the High School Science Room

He's been looking for something simple
like hydrochloric acid or magnesium
for the past half hour, but he's been caught up
by other things: the mummified cat on the top shelf,

the model of a human brain
still tucked away in the model of a human head,
Copernicus, Galileo, Einstein,
bauxite, obsidian, and gypsum.

Passing by the window, there are more
distractions, the varsity football players scuffing each other
in practice, all the weepy-eyed girls
staring astonished as though

these young men could defy physics, like wishes,
to give them anything they want. This will never happen,
but they don't need to know that. A few steps farther,
the clear upside-down

bell of the vacuum chamber waits
for its once a year feeding of balloons and marshmallows,
ready to feast on the air,
drawing it out in one mortifying extended breath.

There is one teacher for all these sections,
a balding minister of a Baptist church,
who tells the boy, quoting a thousand sermons,
he is going to Hell

unless he accepts God into his life.
For a few moments there is a presence
in everything, something blue in the flame
of Bunsen burners, something waiting

in the mongrel pup stored in a jar of formaldehyde,
something in the atoms of helium
that pushes it to float upward toward its own
dispersion. Nothing that holy could exist

on earth. So he resigns himself
to tarsus and metatarsus, tibia and fibula.
The quivering skeleton in the back room
all the kids guess is real,

wondering who it was, and if it suffered,
and, if there are souls in heaven, *is it there?*
But that is another problem, a test
with no observable evidence other than these bones

hanging from a metal pole in the darkness of a storage closet,
ready for its numbered parts to be labeled
and displayed and reassembled.
He could search all afternoon, tomorrow,

and the day after that for whatever it is
he has been sent to find. Outside this room,
he knows the stars are moving farther away.
The light they send is so fleeting and old.

Umbra

Fire starts in the east, morning burn.
It takes hours for this town, this valley
to be scorched away, all this daylight
blazing our patched and broken streets,
all this sunlight withering our good
souls. And before we can fall to ash,
burning shimmers in the west, turning
to embers, shifting as kindling snaps
and breaks and falls into the heat
of dying day. Dying day, and night
is given to ghosts, given freely,
given over to a cheesecloth fog.
I would go out into the night,
but the sepulcher of home ticks
and talks, cracks and balks, calls me
back to heartwood, back to spark
and speck. I will close my eyes
to the ancient light of distant stars.
Give me eight minutes and
an unobstructed view, give me
an explosive heart and a life too long
for memory. Give me a darkness so deep
I can only call out with light.

Resuscitation

I remember a white light.
Or rather warmth and light-headedness,
a dizzying height, a numbness
touching me as though I wasn't there.

I remember falling through clouds,
a feeling of flying, but lost.

Then you were kissing me,
touching my chest,
pressing down upon my heart.

A cat sitting upon a sleeping child
is said to be stealing breath.

I don't know what made me think of that,
unless there is nothing more at 5:03 in the afternoon
but a matter of escaping death,

or something like it.

There's a ringing in my ears.
I've been listening to cicadas
rehearse their songs on a midsummer night,

when changelings wander orchards and fields
looking for souls free from their bodies
to replace them in the living world.

I worry I am not myself.
Stand back.
Give me room.
Let me catch my breath.

Ode to August in the Northern Hemisphere

Storm grass, morning rain hangs from stems.
    Puddles begin a slow ascent from the driveway

back to the sky. Air dances off the street.
    I keep secrets in layers of dust. I can't tell you why.

The garden bestows its bounty into my hands.
    My skin stains and bruises. My back breaks.

All I have to carry is my soul,
    but that is too heavy.

This town is a kiln. Every man, woman, and child comes out
    splintered: icon, image, fetish, figurine.

The gates of Hell fracture.
    My bones are finally warm.

Whisky burns late into the night,
    and lightning flashes on the horizon.

If I were to be born, it would be now.
    It would be early in the morning

when songbirds have nothing better to do.
    If I were to start a life, it would be after

the rain had passed.
    It would be humid. It would be steam
        rising from the cracks of the earth.

Fire Song

Frenetic is my word
      for fire, a wild crackle
          in my bipolar brain.
Thoughts rush through these walls swift
with the speed of light. I stir coals in the wood stove
to see sparks rise like fireflies.
      What a word, so untrue,
          yet so passionate. *Inferno*
is my word for love, a burning
that you can't control. Embers rise and drift,
seethe and sizzle. Something wild can happen,
      can turn your body to ash,
          leave you breathless in the rising
heat. *Sunburst* is my word for mania, a jittery feeling
in the spine. Flames climb fast as angels
      making a run for Heaven,
          knowing sometimes the only end
is otherwise. *Otherwise* is my word for anything
I can't imagine. Which is a burning lie. *Fire*
      is my word for faith,
          my word for knowing something
better burns this tinder, something else
          takes root and grows.

Crows Or Ravens

No one here seems to know the difference, or even care.
All that can be said is that crows are clever,
                    always clever.
They teach their fledglings how to recognize
what can harm and what can kill.

All we know of ravens is just as much—
how close one feather lies next to another.
How difficult it is to see
the difference between unkindness and murder,
impossible to know the subtleties
between storytelling and conspiracy.

I might correct my friends by suggesting
treachery is larger, reminding them
scarecrows are people without souls.

And birds revel with souls, guide us to a flimsy hereafter,
keep us safe on the road from here to where,
                    from this to there.

No one here seems to know rook or jackdaw,
                    midnight or sable.
But sometimes all we have left is forgiveness, a chance
to understand so little of this world is observed,
even as we look to the heavens,
the silhouettes of flight indistinguishable, all of us
                    taking our turns in the sky.

ABOUT THE AUTHOR

David B. Prather's first collection, *We Were Birds*, was published by Main Street Rag Publishing in 2019. Another full-length poetry collection, *Bending Light with Bare Hands*, is forthcoming from Fernwood Press. A past president of West Virginia Writers, Inc., a statewide non-profit organization, he taught English Composition, American Literature, and Creative Writing at West Virginia University at Parkersburg and English Comp at Marietta College in Marietta, Ohio. Prather also served as poetry editor for *Confluence Literary Journal* and for *Tantra Press*, and he hosted the Blennerhassett Reading Series. He currently serves as a reader for *Suburbia Journal*. His poetry, essays, and reviews have appeared in many journals, including *Colorado Review, Seneca Review, Prairie Schooner, The American Journal of Poetry, The Literary Review, Poet Lore*, and many anthologies, including *Voices From the Fierce Intangible World* (from *South Florida Poetry Journal*) and *Endlessly Rocking: Poems in Honor of Walt Whitman's 200th Birthday* (Unbound Content, Englewood, NJ). Prather studied acting at the National Shakespeare Conservatory in New York, and he appeared in a couple of local (West Virginia/Ohio) independent movies. He received his MFA from Warren Wilson College in North Carolina. And he lives in the town where he was born (Parkersburg, West Virginia), where he was recently inducted into the West Virginia Literary Hall of Recognition.

www.ingramcontent.com/pod-product-compliance
Lightning Source LLC
Chambersburg PA
CBHW060339130626
46553CB00003B/1056